T0257039

FANTASIA ON

GREENSLEEVES

ADAPTED FROM THE OPERA

SIR JOHN IN LOVE

R. VAUGHAN WILLIAMS

ARRANGED FOR VIOLA OR VIOLONCELLO AND PIANOFORTE BY

WATSON FORBES

OXFORD UNIVERSITY PRESS

FANTASIA ON
GREENSLEEVES

Arranged for Viola (or Violoncello)
and Pianoforte by
WATSON FORBES

R. VAUGHAN WILLIAMS

Time of Performance 4 mins.

Copyright 1947 Oxford University Press
Printed in Great Britain
OXFORD UNIVERSITY PRESS, MUSIC DEPARTMENT, GREAT CLARENDON STREET, OXFORD OX2 6DP
Photocopying this copyright material is ILLEGAL.

mf
p
p
mf cantabile
rall.

*Folk Tune 'Lovely Joan'

VIOLONCELLO

OXFORD UNIVERSITY PRESS

FANTASIA ON
GREENSLEEVES

Arranged for Viola
and Pianoforte by
WATSON FORBES

R. VAUGHAN WILLIAMS

VIOLA

* The small notes may be omitted

Time of Performance 4 mins.

Copyright 1947 Oxford University Press
Printed in Great Britain
OXFORD UNIVERSITY PRESS, MUSIC DEPARTMENT, GREAT CLARENDON STREET, OXFORD OX2 6DP
Photocopying this copyright material is ILLEGAL.

VIOLA

OXFORD UNIVERSITY PRESS

FANTASIA ON
GREENSLEEVES

Arranged for Violoncello
and Pianoforte by
WATSON FORBES

R. VAUGHAN WILLIAMS

VIOLONCELLO

Time of Performance 4 mins.

Copyright 1947 Oxford University Press
Printed in Great Britain
OXFORD UNIVERSITY PRESS, MUSIC DEPARTMENT, GREAT CLARENDON STREET, OXFORD OX2 6DP
Photocopying this copyright material is ILLEGAL.

pp flautando
mf
p
cresc.
f
Cadenza
dim. e rall.
cresc.
f

Lento
p
pp
Lento moderato
mp
p
cantabile
pp
p
mf
cantabile

Reproduced and printed by
Halstan & Co. Ltd., Amersham, Bucks., England

OXFORD UNIVERSITY PRESS